LITTLE BOOKS OF FLOWERS:

- Dahlias
- Peonies
- Tulips

Camano Sitka

Dahlias

A LITTLE BOOK OF FLOWERS

Tara Austen Weaver

Illustrations by Emily Poole

SASQUATCH BOOKS
SEATTLE

For Lian,
Who cultivates gardens, people, books, and dogs
I am so lucky to have fallen into your orbit
Some family you inherit, some family you choose
Thank you for being my chosen.

Beware the dahlia; this flower possesses a bewitching beauty with a penchant for stealing the hearts of gardeners.

—SHANNON McCABE

Polka

Contents

Origin of the Species 8

Forms of the Flower 14

Dahlia Growing &
Flower Culture 54

Making the Most of
Dahlias 84

Flower Viewing 100

Glossary 121
Pests & Diseases 127
Resources 137

Origin of the Species

There's probably no plant in the flower kingdom that gives the gardener more spectacular reward than the dahlia.

—RAY ALLEN

Dahlias are the showgirls of the flower world—extravagantly beautiful, they sashay into the summer garden and demand all our attention. But like any stage performer, their beauty is deceptive. Dahlias are hard workers and strong, putting out bloom after bloom from midsummer right into autumn. The show finally ends with the first hard frost, which brings down the curtain on their dazzling performance. Few flowers produce for so long, with such diversity of color, size, shape, and cutting potential. If ever there was a bloom that earned its keep, it's the dahlia.

The modern dahlia traces its roots to Mexico and Central America, where they were cultivated and gathered wild by the Aztecs and other indigenous people, prized more for their edible roots and hollow stems that were used to carry water than for the flowers themselves. The name for dahlias in the Nahuatl language spoken by the Aztecs is *acocoxo-chitl*, which translates as "water tube flower." Dahlia root tubers were also used for their curative properties—to treat ailments such as epilepsy, fevers, urinary tract disorders, and colic. The petals were known to soothe rashes, insect bites, and dry skin.

When European explorers arrived from Spain in the late 1500s, they were intrigued by the flowers they saw growing wild on sunny hillsides. The blooms were fairly simple, with a single row of petals, but all attention was focused on the tubers—plump underground roots that resembled a sweet potato in shape. The first drawings of what we know as dahlias were published in Europe in 1651.

D. Merckii

By the late eighteenth century dahlias themselves had arrived in Europe—sent by the director of the Botanical Garden in Mexico City to the Royal Botanical Garden of Madrid, where they were named for the famous Swedish botanist Anders Dahl. Initial interest in the edibility of the tubers quickly faded (they are fibrous and can cause digestive upset), but this era was marked by great botanical exploration, where European botanical gardens, noted horticulturists, and the aristocracy were vying to acquire the rare plants that were being brought from all corners of the globe. By the early 1800s, dahlias had made their way to France and England, eagerly sought after and in high demand. The flowers were still quite simple, but that soon was to change.

The 1800s saw a frenzy of dahlia introductions across Europe—the anemone dahlia was developed in Ireland, while the charming collarette emerged in France, and the formal decorative in Germany. The spiky cactus form was introduced by the Dutch, the lone surviving dahlia tuber from a crate that had been shipped from Mexico but rotted during the journey. Dahlias became a hobby of the wealthy (or, rather, the work of their gardeners). Tubers could be purchased but they were not cheap, and flower shows offered generous prizes for exciting new blooms.

As growers throughout Europe began breeding dahlias, more decorative blooms were developed. By 1836, the Horticultural Society of London (now the Royal Horticultural Society) published a dahlia register that listed seven hundred different varieties of the flower. The year prior had seen forty-five different dahlia shows held in Britain alone. Dahlia fever was taking hold.

The Great Exhibition, held in London in 1851, put the dahlia on the map in a new way, introducing it to a wider cross-section of society and increasing demand. The upper classes had been installing "dahlia walks" in their gardens—grassy paths lined with wide beds of dahlias so they could admire the blooms—but now the average backyard gardener wanted dahlias as well. Dahlias were said to symbolize dignity to the Victorians, with their upright stalks, though the meaning broadened over time to include elegance, respect, compassion, and a lifelong bond.

Part of the success of the dahlia is due to how easy they are to hybridize. Most dahlias are grown from tubers, resulting in an exact clone of the original flower. By collecting and planting the seed of any dahlia, however, you will grow a combination of the original dahlia and whatever dahlia whose pollen was brought by bees or other pollinators. As a result, there are more than fifty thousand named cultivars of dahlias, with more being introduced each year.

This excitement for dahlias continues today—in new varieties that are released to the public, in the delight of seeing the first bloom of a new cultivar in the garden, in the generosity of a plant that starts off in midsummer and blooms until frost takes it down, in the fact that cutting flowers is a sure way to encourage more blooms. It's no wonder that people so easily become obsessed with the dahlia.

Forms of the Flower

The last summer flower
   to bloom
is the dahlia, sassy as a
   French mob cap,
insistent as a harvest moon.

—BRYN GRIBBEN

Dahlia Botany

Dahlias are members of the Asteraceae family (formerly called the Compositae family). This large family includes other single-petal, open-center flowers such as cosmos, rudbeckias, and the common daisy.

Dahlias grow from underground tubers (fleshy storage roots), sprouting in late spring and growing into bush-like plants. The leaves range in color from green to a dark-eggplant color (though the latter is much less common).

Dahlia flowers offer a range of different forms, sizes, and colors. The palette for dahlias is similarly deep and wide. The only color that has not been successfully cultivated is blue, though breeders have spent years trying.

While the different dahlia forms vary widely, the single-flowered dahlia consists of a center disk that is formed of short, tubular florets. The disk is surrounded by a row of eight ray florets. Below the disk lies the flower's ovary. A long style grows from the ovary and divides into two stigmas at its tip. The style is surrounded by anthers, which split open to release pollen.

This section will introduce you to each of the dahlia forms and suggest some recommended cultivars—though with thousands to choose from, this is of course an incomplete list. Consider this merely an entry point into the wide world of dahlias.

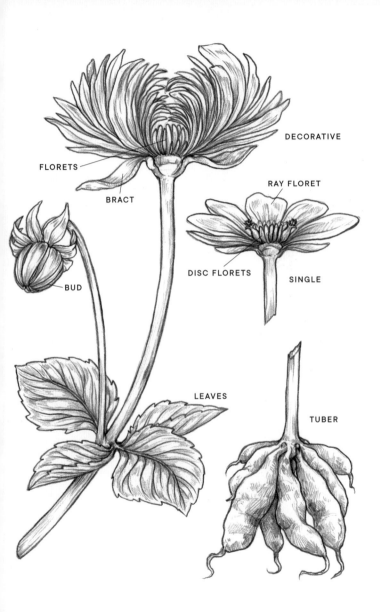

DECORATIVE

FLORETS

BRACT

RAY FLORET

DISC FLORETS

SINGLE

BUD

LEAVES

TUBER

SINGLE

CACTUS

BALL

INFORMAL
DECORATIVE

COLLARETTE

ANEMONE

PEONY

FORMAL
DECORATIVE

ORCHID

WATERLILY

Single and Mignon

The simplest of all dahlia forms, singles have a row of petals—usually eight—circling an open center made up of disk florets (similar to the yellow center of a daisy). Popular with pollinators and prolific bloomers, singles are an asset to any garden.

Mignon singles are similar to single dahlias but have rounded petal tips and measure less than 2 inches across; think of them as mini-singles.

Single

'Magenta Star'
A darker pink single variety with a center that is reddish brown with gold fringe, this is a prolific bloomer. The flowers look as if they are floating on long stems above a mass of foliage so dark green it almost verges on brown.

'Chocolate Sundae'
This one's a stunner: dark-maroon petals look velvety as they surround a slightly shaggy golden center. The dark-green foliage grows only 2 feet, making this an eye-catching front of border plant.

Mignon

'Bambino'
A sweet, daisylike bloom with creamy white rounded petals circling a golden button-like center. They grow to only 1 foot, so tuck them in the front of borders or planting beds, or grow in a pot for deck-side attraction.

Magenta Star

Chocolate Sundae

Bambino

Cactus, Semi-cactus, Incurved Cactus, and Laciniated

Known for narrow petals that roll outward forming a spiky, starlike bloom, the cactus dahlia family provides an eye-catching sense of geometry in the garden. Cactus forms have straight, rolled petals, while semi-cactus flowers have petals that are broader at the bottom and roll toward the tip, providing a slight swoop. Incurved cactus petals are spiky but curve back toward the center, creating a much greater sense of motion and excitement, sometimes looking spidery. Laciniated dahlias resemble the cactus form, with the same spiky, rolled petals, but each petal forks at the tip; the effect is a little like floral fireworks.

Cactus

'Brookside Cheri'
A standout in the late-summer garden, this cactus dahlia features salmon-pink flowers with spiky cactus petals and touches of yellow in the center. The 6-inch blooms grow on a 4-foot-tall bush with strong laterals and stems, adding a cheerful note to garden beds.

Brookside Cheri

Semi-cactus

'Wildcat'
With its brilliant yellow base and red-tipped petals, this
dahlia is a bright spot in the garden. It has midsize blooms
of 3½ inches with slightly curved petals. The bush measures
up to 4½ feet tall. An excellent option for autumnal flower
arrangements and bouquets.

Incurved Cactus

'Bed Head'
This charmingly named dahlia looks exactly as you would
imagine: a mass of incurved orange petals that wave like wild
hair. Its 4-inch tangerine blooms grow on strong stems, but
place this one toward the back of the garden, as it can grow
as tall as 6 feet.

Laciniated

'Citron Du Cap'
Clouds of white-yellow blooms float above pale green stems.
The forked laciniated petals have the faintest hint of laven-
der at the tips, giving an ethereal glow to the 7-inch blooms.
A popular show flower, it grows on a 4-foot bush and looks
like a feathery pompom.

Wildcat

Bed Head

Citron Du Cap

Ball, Miniature Ball, and Pompon

Ball dahlias are visual marvels—perfectly round, filled with regularly placed petals, either blunt or slightly rounded at the tips. Miniature balls measure 2 to 3½ inches, while pompon dahlias are even smaller—under 2 inches.

Ball and Miniature Ball

'Crichton Honey'
There are many beautiful colors of ball dahlias, but this one is truly special: a mix of apricot and pinkish gold that comes alight when hit by the late afternoon sun. These 4-inch balls glow tawny pink in the garden and look just as appealing in a vase.

'Camano Zoe'
A favorite of wedding designers, this miniature ball blooms in cream blushed with the palest pink and a center that glows with a tinge of yellow. Spherical 3-inch flowers seem to float on 4-foot plants; they look elegant in the garden or in a vase or bouquet.

Pompon

'Frank Holmes'
Pompon dahlias are tiny, almost unreal versions of ball dahlias, and this is one of the most charming. These petite lavender flowers look almost quilted—the regular perfection of their petals is mesmerizing. Since they measure only 1½ inches, tuck these flowers at the front of a border or garden bed.

Crichton Honey

Frank Holmes

Decorative (Formal and Informal) and Stellar

Decorative dahlias are double flowers with broad, blunt-tipped petals that curve back toward the stem. Formal decorative dahlias feature evenly placed petals, while informal decorative dahlias have flat petals that roll at the tips with a slight waviness. Stellar dahlias are similar to other decorative flowers, but each petal is slightly creased in a way that causes them to narrow and curve backward, providing a sense of motion, somewhat like a shooting star.

Formal Decorative

'All That Jazz'
A raspberry delight, this dahlia showcases the pleasing regularity of the formal decorative style. Each petal is edged in pale pink and white, adding interest and depth. It produces flowers with slight variations—touches of gold and yellow here and there, and a range of colors from magenta to pink and hints of orange. These 5-inch blooms brighten up any garden and quickly become a favorite flower.

All That Jazz

Informal Decorative

'Café au Lait'
The undisputed queen of the dahlia garden, this cultivar has become a major fan favorite in recent years, with large, 8-inch flowers that resemble flourishes of frosting. Popular with brides and wedding designers, these dahlias run from ivory and cream to palest pink and lavender. A late-season bloomer, these sought-after flowers are eagerly awaited. It is often referred to as a dinnerplate dahlia due to its large size, but it technically is an informal decorative. These irregular blooms won't win prizes at the dahlia show, but that hardly matters when they win so many hearts.

Stellar

'Dancin' Queen'
This stellar dahlia takes the stage in a pink flash, its petals curving back into a poof that will brighten your garden. These 7-inch candy-pink blooms rise above a 5-foot bush like a shooting star with a bit of gold in their center.

Café au Lait

Dancin' Queen

Collarette

One of the most charming of the dahlia forms, collarettes feature an outer ring of broad, flat petals that surround an inner row of shorter petals around a flat center—a ruff-like collar, if you will. The contrasting colors between the rows of petals gives a sense of whimsy to the flowers.

Collarette

'Apple Blossom'
Like the freshness of a spring day, this collarette sallies forth with buttery peach petals that fade to blush and a pale-pink collar surrounding a gold button center. A favorite flower for bridal bouquets, backyard gardeners, and bees that love the open centers, these 4-inch beauties perch on top of 4½-foot bushes, looking a bit like butterflies in the garden.

'Bumble Rumble'
This dahlia is long on charm. An unusually thick collar of creamy white inner petals radiates out from a dark-golden center and creates a ruff, while outer petals streaked in raspberry-pink with rounded tips peek out from behind. The improbable combination demands attention, instantly drawing the eye to these colorful, 3-inch blooms.

Apple Blossom

Bumble Rumble

Anemone and Peony

Anemone dahlias feature a ring of flat petals surrounding a pincushion of small, elongated florets in the center that resemble a fluffy mound. The surrounding petals may be a single row or more. Peony dahlias, on the other hand, have an open center surrounded by two to five rows of petals, which are slightly cupped. This gives the flower a fluffy, somewhat rumpled look.

Anemone

'Lambada'
These anemone dahlias look like a pale sunset—a creamy pink pincushion with hints of yellow, darkest at the center, surrounded by petals of dusty rose. These 4-inch stunners provide texture in the garden and in the vase; their unusual form is sure to garner attention.

Peony

'Bishop of Canterbury'
This peony dahlia is lovely—two rows of bright-plum petals surround a textured center of gold and rusty red. These 4-inch flowers wave over finely cut dark foliage on stems the color of eggplants. This is one of a series of peony-type dahlias known for their attractive dark leaves: 'Bishop of Oxford' blooms with coppery-orange petals, 'Bishop of York' is golden, and 'Bishop of Llandaff' is an eye-catching bright scarlet.

Lambada

Bishop of Canterbury

Novelty Open and Novelty Double

Novelty is bit of a catch-all category that encompasses flowers that don't neatly fit into other classifications. Novelty open flowers have open centers and petals that are proportional to the center. Novelty fully double flowers have closed centers and good symmetry.

Novelty Open

'Junkyard Dog'
The dark-raspberry center streaks on the petals pale to lighter pink on each side, an unusual pattern. Each petal of the stunning 7-inch bloom slims to a sharp point. The 5-foot-tall plants are an eye catcher in the garden and in arrangements of all kinds.

Novelty Double

'Valley Porcupine'
One of the most unusual of the novelty double dahlias, this variety features creamy petals that are quilled, each pink edge curving toward the other so the flower feels a little prickly to the touch. These 3-inch blooms are popular with wedding designers.

Junkyard Dog

Valley Porcupine

Orchid, Double Orchid, and Orchette

Orchid dahlias look like a series of stars. They feature eight petals that roll, forming the spikes of a star surrounding a yellow or golden open center. Orchette dahlias are similar but have an additional petaloid collar around the center (like the collarettes). While quite simple—especially when compared to most other dahlia forms—a constellation of stars floating on long stems adds a touch of magic to your garden at twilight. Double orchid dahlias also exist; the second row of petals gives them more of a tassel or loose pompom look.

Orchid and Double Orchid

- 'NTAC Shelly' (orchid: 4 inch, 3½ feet)
- 'Pink Giraffe' (double orchid: 4 inch, 3 feet)

Orchette

- 'Verrone's Morning Star' (3 inch, 4 feet)

Pink Giraffe

Verrone's Morning Star   NTAC Shelly

Waterlily

This closed-center dahlia features broad, shallow petals that curve inward at the tips, resembling its namesake, the waterlily. Though waterlily dahlias tend to have strong stems, the flowers sometimes nod downward due to size; they look stunning, however, floating in a shallow bowl of water.

'Pam Howden'
Long a favorite of dahlia show competitors, this flower is a winner in so many ways. A gold center radiates out into peach, orange, and pink in this classic, 4-inch waterlily style that lights up in the late afternoon sun.

'Snowflake'
Snowflakes of summer—these pristine waterlily blooms decorate 5-foot bushes, suspended on strong stems that make for excellent cut flowers with a long vase life. Deservedly popular with brides, wedding designers, and those who are fond of all-white gardens, Snowflake will happily bloom all summer long.

Pam Howden

Snowflake

DAHLIA SIZE CLASSIFICATIONS

While the dahlia forms cover the shape of a flower, because of the great diversity in dahlias, we must also mention size classifications. These certainly come into play with competitive flower shows. Here are the official American Dahlia Society guidelines.

AA: Giant, 10 inches in diameter

A: Large, between 8 and 10 inches in diameter

B: Medium, between 6 and 8 inches in diameter

BB: Small, between 4 and 6 inches in diameter

M: Miniature, up to 4 inches in diameter

BA: Ball, more than 3½ inches in diameter

MB: Miniature ball, between 2 and 3½ inches in diameter

P: Pompon, up to 2 inches in diameter

MS: Mignon single, up to 2 inches in diameter

S: Single, more than 2 inches in diameter

Dahlia Growing & Flower Culture

There is nothing like the first hot days of spring when the gardener stops wondering if it's too soon to plant the dahlias and starts wondering if it's too late.

—HENRY MITCHELL

Preparing to Plant

While it is possible to grow dahlias from their seeds, most backyard growers start off the spring by planting tubers—beige-brown fleshy roots, several inches long, that vaguely resemble sweet potatoes. Once planted, these tubers will sprout from the buds (called eyes) that are located at the point where the tuber joins the stem of the dahlia that bloomed the previous summer. Depending on how many eyes a tuber has, there may be multiple stems sprouting from the same dahlia tuber.

Whether you store them yourself, order them from a commercial grower, or receive them from a friend, tubers should not be wrinkled, discolored, or rotten. They may be small and skinny, or large and plump; each are capable of growing strong stems and flowers. If your tuber has been in storage a while, it may have started sprouting on its own. This is fine, just trim any tender shoots that may have developed back to 1 inch from the tuber. This will help prevent weak shoot growth. If a shoot breaks off during planting, do not despair; it will likely grow back. In fact, avid dahlia growers and nursery professionals often cut off emerging new sprouts and root them separately to make new plants and thus increase their stock of dahlias.

PURCHASING DAHLIA TUBERS

If your dahlia purchase has been grown in the United States or Canada, you will most likely receive a single tuber that resembles a small sweet potato or finger of ginger. International growers, however, tend to sell their tubers as first-year clumps grown from cuttings—often they will be packaged two or three clumps in a bag. A clump consists of a main stem with a number of small tubers branching off.

While both the single tubers and clumps can produce blooms, the clumps are sometimes damaged during shipping, with slender necks broken and tubers dangling (these should be cut off). Even with this damage, you should be able to salvage viable tubers, but a package of three clumps will not always yield three dahlia plants. Seeking out local growers, many of whom guarantee their tubers, often results in a more reliable product. Regional dahlia association chapters will also frequently host tuber sales each spring; these local tubers may be more reliable than imported options.

Planting Dahlias

To get your dahlias off to a good start, make sure to pick the best location for them and prepare the soil well. Dahlias need full sun—8 hours or more is ideal, unless you are growing in a particularly hot climate where it may be better to have some shade during the heat of the day. Because dahlias grow on slender stems, select a sheltered location that does not get significant winds.

Dahlias prefer rich, well-draining soil that is slightly acidic (pH 6.5–7.0). A few weeks before planting, dig in about 2 inches of compost or aged manure from a trusted source. If your soil is heavy or claylike, add some organic matter, sand, or peat moss to lighten it up and help with drainage. If dahlia tubers are planted in soil that is too heavy and does not drain well, they may rot.

Dahlias should be planted out in April or May, depending on your climate (a good rule of thumb is to aim for Mother's Day). The tuber won't begin to grow until the soil reaches 60 degrees F (15 degrees C), so there's no point in rushing it— tubers planted out before the weather warms will not thrive. Those who live in cooler climates often start tubers indoors in pots or growing flats to get a jump on the season.

For each tuber to be planted, dig a 6-inch hole and amend it with a small handful of bone meal, mixing in with the native soil. Plant each tuber at the bottom of the hole, placed horizontally on its side with the largest eye pointed upward. If you are growing one of the taller cultivars (4 foot and above), now is the time to put a stake in place to be able to tie up the tall stalk and prevent it from toppling over.

Position a stake (4 or 5 feet tall) so the tuber end with the eyes is pointing in the opposite direction of the stake, to allow room for new tuber growth. Pound the stake in about 1 foot and make sure it is firmly in the ground with no wiggling.

Backfill the soil over the tuber and tamp down firmly. It is not recommended to water dahlias when planting, as the excess moisture may cause them to rot. Dahlias should not be watered until the first shoots appear.

Space dahlias 2 to 3 feet apart to allow for airflow and root growth—bedding dahlias, which are small, can be spaced 1 foot apart. Larger flowers need 3 feet or more. Do not mulch dahlias, as this only provides habitat for slugs and snails.

Dahlia Maintenance

A few weeks after planting your tubers, start monitoring for shoots breaking through the soil. This is your cue to lay down slug bait—or you may not want to wait for shoots to appear if you have a slug-filled garden. Slugs and snails love to eat new, tender dahlia growth. In most cases, this will not destroy your dahlias, but losing new growth will delay their eventual bloom. Continue to lay down slug bait for the first month or so, especially after any rains. Once the dahlia stems grow taller and toughen up, they are less appealing to these pests. Continue to monitor throughout the season, however, as leaf damage may indicate high-climbing slugs and snails. Some slug bait also wards off earwigs and cut-worms (though if you have children, cats and/or dogs, make sure to buy a formula that is child and pet safe).

Once the dahlia shoots are visible, you can begin to water. Dahlias need consistent watering as the season progresses. Plan to water deeply 2 to 3 times a week, depending on your climate and weather. Soil should be kept moderately damp, but never soggy.

Fertilizer can be applied starting after sprouting and continuing through the summer, about once a month. Use a low-nitrogen, slow-release fertilizer (5-10-10 or 10-20-20 or 3-9-5, for example). Low nitrogen—which is indicated by the first number—is important, as an excess will result in more foliage growth than flowers. Don't fertilize after August, as the dahlias won't have time to take up the nutrition before the end of the season and the tubers will not store as well.

When dahlias have grown about 1 foot tall and have put out three to four sets of leaves, it's recommended to snip out the center growing tip, just above a set of leaves. This will cause the plant to grow two stalks on either side of the cut stem and encourages lateral branching; it results in a shorter, bushier plant. This will also delay your first blooms by a bit. If you are eager for early blooms, or prefer taller, less bushy plants, you can choose not to snip. Experiment to see what you like best.

Another trick practiced by some dahlia growers is disbudding—removing the two side buds in a cluster. This will lead to larger flowers, as the plant puts all its energy into the main bloom. Disbudding is often used by those who are growing dahlias for competition, to encourage large, show-stopping blooms.

Begin tying taller dahlias to their stakes when they've reached about knee height (a loose circle of twine will do the trick). It's also good to keep an eye on larger flowers, especially in summer rain or wind storms. They may need extra support, or to have their waterlogged flowers or bent stems trimmed off.

Dahlia flowers need to be cut, as this encourages more buds to flower. Either cut them in full bloom to enjoy or give away, or deadhead (cut and remove) spent blossoms once they've begun to wither on the bush. Cut the stem just above a lower set of double leaves or branching stems to stimulate the next set of buds to open. Dahlias truly are a plant that keeps on giving.

Dahlias will bloom prolifically into autumn, though they eventually begin to look a bit bedraggled (it's not uncommon for powdery mildew to set in late in the season). Still, it's a pleasure to have flowers and color as the garden winds down from the summer. The first hard frost, however, will reduce dahlias to a sad, dark, and sodden mess. This means it is time to clean up for the winter.

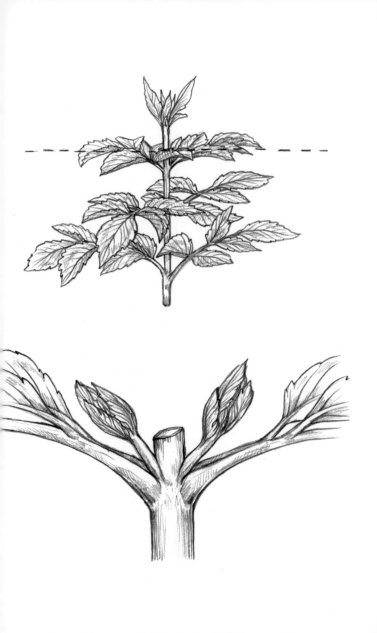

Pests and Diseases

Dahlias are fairly easy to grow—one of those plants that produces flowers for months with minimal upkeep. It is possible to prevent most disease issues with good growing practices—plant in areas with adequate sunlight and drainage, and space your dahlias for good airflow. If you do run into challenges, however, check the Pest & Diseases section (page 127) for help in diagnosing the issue and advice on treating it.

Dahlias in Winter

In cold climates, where the ground freezes solid (Zone 7 and lower), dahlia tubers must be dug and stored over the winter and planted out again in the spring. Some people prefer to treat dahlias like annuals and repurchase tubers each spring, as digging and storing dahlias does require effort and strategy—not to mention the storage space. This is a perfectly fine solution, if you don't mind the ongoing expense, and may be the right one for you, but it means you'll miss out on one of the best features of the dahlia—increasing your supply of tubers to plant or give away.

Each dahlia tuber, as it grows and blooms over the summer season, produces more fingerlike tubers growing off the main stem. By digging up and dividing your dahlias, you can significantly increase the number of tubers you have each year. Even those living in warmer climates who do not need to dig their tubers for winter storage can dig them in the early spring to divide and increase their yield.

While technically dahlias are considered hardy to Zone 8, this is not an absolutely reliable fact. If your soil is heavy and claylike, if you have poor drainage, and if you get a lot of rain, you may want to dig your tubers, even if you live in Zone 8. The danger is that they may rot over the winter, so assess the level of risk your situation presents and make your decisions accordingly.

If you decide to not dig your tubers in fall, cut down their stalks and remove any foliage debris that might provide harbor to pests or diseases. Cut the stalks down to about 1 inch below the soil line (to the point where the stalk's hollow center is filled in). A hollow stalk, if left in place, will act like a straw and funnel rainwater into your tuber, which can then rot or freeze and cause damage. And because cutting all your stems at the same time with the same tool can spread disease from one dahlia to another, make sure to clean your clippers between plants with a solution of one part bleach to nine parts water.

Protect tubers left in the ground over winter by mulching heavily with leaves or straw and a layer of compost before the ground freezes. Some gardeners give added protection by covering the soil with sheets of plastic to reduce the moisture level in that area. Adding mulch, leaves, or other insulating materials on top of the plastic may provide a little extra protection (and will help disguise the plastic in your garden). Remove the plastic in early spring, once risk of freezing has passed, and take away any mulch that might harbor slugs and snails.

Digging up Tubers

To dig tubers in fall, wait until your area has experienced a killing frost and the dahlia greens have wilted and turned black. After that hard frost, cut the stalks down to about 4 inches; this encourages the tuber skins to thicken and toughen a bit. Give the tubers a week or so to winterize before digging them up. If there is rain in your forecast, however, cover the stems so that water does not fill them up. You can use a tarp, a plastic bag, kitchen foil, or plastic wrap to cover each stem to prevent rain from getting in. This is also a good time to mark your tubers with a plant tag around the stem noting the name of the cultivar, so they don't get mixed up when digging (some growers use a bit of plastic ribbon or even painter's tape and a waterproof marker).

To lift your tubers, clear off a bit of the soil from around the stem and loosen up what remains, but don't dig deeper than 1 or 2 inches. Next, loosen the soil in a large circle about 1 foot out from the tuber area. (If you are digging up an older tuber that has not been divided recently, start further out.) Gently loosen the soil by driving a shovel or pitchfork into the soil and wiggling the handle back and forth. Then, slowly and carefully guide the shovel or pitchfork under the tuber clump and lift it up from the bottom, shaking off as much dirt as possible.

Let the tubers sit several hours after digging and they will be easier to clean. Make sure to mark each clump by name, however, if you haven't tagged them already. Tubers easily become mixed up once dug from their planting site; the clumps look quite similar.

Cut the stem down to 1 inch or so and turn the clump upside down to wash off with a strong stream of water. If any of the tuber fingers have been damaged or sliced open in the digging process, cut them off the main clump at their narrow neck with sharp clippers and discard. Also cut off the narrow, tail-like ends of the tubers and any hairy feeder roots.

Tubers can be divided immediately after lifting from the garden in the fall (see instructions, page 71). At this point the tubers themselves are tender and easy to cut, but the eyes—the growth buds for the next season—are harder to see. If you do want to divide in fall, do not delay; tuber eyes will be most visible in the first 48 hours after being dug up. Otherwise, let the tubers dry a few days before preparing them for storage and wait to divide them in the spring.

If you are new to dahlia dividing, you may want to wait until spring when the eyes are getting ready to sprout and are more obvious. If the tuber clumps are too large to be easily stored, you can simply cut them in half or in quarters—straight down through the stem from top to bottom. This way you have smaller clumps to deal with. You can divide them into individual tubers in the spring—or even plant them out in half or quarter pieces if you do not yet feel confident in locating the eyes. Make sure to let your tubers sit out for 2 or 3 days after cutting, in a cool and dry place, so all cuts seal before being packed up for storage.

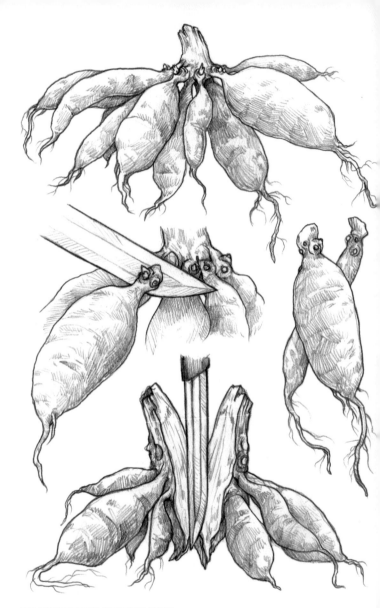

SPLITTING TUBER CLUMP IN HALF

As another level of protection from rot, some growers like to dip their tubers in a solution of one part bleach to nine parts water. This can be done after digging the tubers if you plan to store them intact, or after dividing if you choose to do that in the fall.

Storing Tubers

Because climate and storage circumstances vary widely, there is no single right way to store dahlia tubers for winter—the trick is finding what works for you and your particular situation. When starting out, try several different methods—both to figure out what works best, but also to increase your chance of success by not putting all your eggs—or tubers, rather—in one basket. It's a certain sort of heartbreak to lose all your dahlias and have to start over.

The goal is to keep tubers at a moderately cool and steady temperature—the ideal range is 40 to 50 degrees F (4–10 degrees C). Dry conditions will cause tubers to dehydrate and shrivel. If it is too cold or damp, they will freeze or rot.

In order to insulate tubers, dahlias should be stored in some sort of packing material. What is the best material is a matter hotly contested by dahlia growers. With a little time and experimentation, everyone seems to find their favorite. Here are the most popular options.

- **Peat moss:** if purchased new it can be used straight out of the sealed bag. If using an older bag—or reusing material from previous years—you may need to mist with water for adequate moisture. Mix for even distribution of moisture. The goal is ever so slightly damp, never soggy.
- **Vermiculite:** comes packed dry, so it will need added moisture. If you are using a new bag, spray lightly with water and mix throughout.
- **Wood shavings:** some dahlia growers warn off using cedar shavings, others seem to have no problem with them. If there is too much moisture in your packed dahlias, however, woodchips are known to rot.
- **Plastic wrap:** Another method is to wrap each divided tuber in plastic wrap (a tutorial for this can be found on the American Dahlia Society website).

No matter the packing material you use, however, never store tubers in zip-top plastic bags, or anything with an airtight seal. This will lead to rot.

As for what to store your tubers and packing materials in, there is a variety of options. Some people use cardboard boxes lined with newspaper, others use plastic bulb crates or wooden crates, or plastic container bins. Some growers protect their tubers from fluctuation in temperature by storing them in an insulated cooler—the sort used for camping trips and cookouts—with the lid cracked slightly open for ventilation, not clasped.

The third variable is where to store your containers of dahlias. Garage, basement, or garden shed are all common choices. Again, it depends on the specifics of your situation and climate. If your garage temperature fluctuates, or if your garden shed freezes, they are not good options. Find a place where you are most likely to get a consistently cool temperature that is not terribly moist or dry. Some people store their tubers in the refrigerator or a commercial cooler, where they can have more control of the conditions.

Note: because many backyard dahlia growers do store their tubers in a garage, remember that a concrete floor will absorb moisture. It's best to put your crates or boxes of tubers up on something—like metal racking or a wooden pallet—so they are not sitting directly on the floor.

It's also important to check your tubers monthly to see how they are doing (you don't need to check each tuber, just an overall spot check). Shriveling tubers means they are dehydrating and need to be misted with water from a spray bottle. Rot means they are either too moist or have been frozen. Keep an eye on them so you can address problems as they develop and prevent large-scale loss.

Dividing Dahlias

The most important thing when dividing dahlias is to look for the eyes, or growth buds (see page 68). These are found around the base of the stem from the previous year's bloom (imagine the tubers as a skirt flaring out from the stem; the eyes would be found in the waistband area). Each tuber needs at least one eye to be viable. If you cut the tuber off the stem without an eye, it won't grow, no matter how plump and healthy it might look.

What do eyes look like? Sometimes they don't look like much. You may need some practice to be able to find them with ease. When you do find them, they'll look a little like tiny pimples—just a small series of bumps.

If it's hard to see the eyes, try using a finger and gently running it over the area between the tuber neck and the stem. Dahlia eyes have a different texture than the stem— somewhat like the tip of an eraser. With practice, however, eyes become much easier to see. If you wait until spring to do tuber division, the eyes will be quite obvious—some of them may have begun to swell or sprout already. Spring tubers that have been stored will be tougher, however, and harder to cut.

Not every tuber will have an eye. Some tubers grow off other tubers—they may look strong, but if they are not attached to the stem and do not have an eye, they will not sprout when planted. Other tubers may be too small to flourish. It's best to go through and remove these nonviable tubers before attempting final division.

Using garden snips or a knife, begin to remove tubers with visible eyes. As you do this, you will encounter the mother tuber—usually slightly darker than the others, with tougher skin; it may be located in the center or at the bottom of the tuber clump. The mother tuber is the one that was planted the previous spring. Most people discard the mother tuber, but if you want to keep it, they generally will sprout another year.

Once the outer tubers are removed it can get difficult to do the final division. If you find it too nerve-wracking, consider splitting the clump through the center, right down the middle of the stem. Make sure to allow all cut surfaces to seal over 2 or 3 days before packing up for winter storage (or for planting, if dividing in the spring).

How to Hybridize

The great diversity in the dahlia genus is due to genetics. While most living organisms are diploids—possessing two sets of chromosomes, one from each parent—dahlias are octoploids. This means they have eight sets of chromosomes. The variety that can arise from such complexity is exciting and full of potential. While there are many who love growing dahlias for exactly what they are—a wide range of gorgeous flowers—some are drawn to the possibility of creating unique dahlia crosses through hybridizing their blooms. Each year brings exciting new dahlia cultivars that are released by professional and amateur breeders alike.

On its face, hybridizing new flower forms appears simple. Each dahlia flower, when pollinated, will produce seed. If this seed is collected, dried, and planted out the next spring, the flower that grows will be a genetic combination of the flower that produced the seed—called the seed parent—and the flower whose pollen was carried in by a bee or other pollinator that visited both blooms.

If you want to experiment with hybridizing, you can simply allow a few dahlia flower heads to dry on the stalk (don't deadhead them). Once fully dry, pull open the flower head to collect the seed. The seeds will be black if they are mature. Make sure they are completely dry before storing and plant in early spring the next year. Dahlia seeds should be started indoors in March or April, depending on your climate (about 6 weeks before you are ready to plant outside).

seeds

COLLECTING SEEDS

The problem with this method is that it's not precise and likely won't lead to anything special in the flower department. You could get lucky, but the odds are against it. Breeders say that only one out of a thousand dahlia crosses will be worth saving.

This is also due to genetics. When it comes to dahlias, single petals, small flowers, tall stems, and downward-facing blooms are all dominant. An unintentional cross is likely to retreat toward the appearance of the original species or wild dahlias—an open-center flower with a single row of petals. All the fancy flowers we've come to love are the result of centuries of careful selection and intentional breeding to make more elaborate blooms. If you want to develop anything that looks like a modern dahlia, it pays to be more selective about hybridizing.

The techniques used by breeders for crossing dahlias are varied. Some will plant only the dahlias that have the traits they are hoping to foster—or cull their garden so that only certain flowers remain. Once the flowers with desirable traits have been isolated, the bees are allowed to do their work in the hopes of a favorable result. Sometimes this technique is used within a closed greenhouse system, where only plants the breeder hopes to cross are planted (bees may need to be intentionally added to this system).

Breeders who want more control over the process will often pollinate by hand. This requires creating a barrier around the flower to be pollinated, so you can be in control of what pollen gets in. Breeders will use tulle or organza, often crafted into small, drawstring bags, to go over the flower head. This allows sunlight to penetrate, but not the pollinators.

TULLE POLLINATOR BARRIER

POLLINATING BY PAINTBRUSH

When put in place before the flower bud has opened, a barrier will protect the dahlia from inadvertent pollination. This is done to both flowers that are to be crossed. Once the flowers have bloomed, the breeder will collect pollen from one bloom and—using a dry and clean paintbrush—carefully apply it to the other flower. This is done several times in hopes of a successful cross. You'll have to wait until the following summer to see what has been created—and it is this excitement and potential that keeps breeders trying.

Show Flowers

Once a dahlia grower has created a new hybrid, how does it go from their garden or growing fields to wider distribution? Some people grow just for themselves and to share tubers with friends and family. Others may sell their tubers direct to customers—there are many small, independently owned dahlia growers (you can find a listing in the resources section at the back of this book). Some people, however, are interested in formal recognition for their new hybrid and wider commercial distribution. This is accomplished via the American Dahlia Society (ADS).

The American Dahlia Society was founded in 1915 to support and encourage interest in dahlia growing. Today it encompasses seventy chapters throughout the United States and Canada, which meet regularly to promote education and development of the flowers. They also are in charge of publishing the annual Classification and Handbook of Dahlias (CHD), which lists officially named cultivars of the flower.

In addition to their publications, one of the main activities of ADS is to plan and host an annual dahlia show and competition at the height of bloom season—there is a national show, as well as regional shows sponsored by local chapters. This is an opportunity to educate attendees who might be interested in growing, and to allow members and visitors to show off and be rewarded for their hard work and expertise. This is also where breeders can introduce new dahlias to the world, by entering them to be evaluated by judges trained by the ADS.

It's worth noting that ADS has strong ideas as to what makes a "good" dahlia. Their website lists the criteria—including specifics such as angle of flower head to stem. This doesn't mean a dahlia that fails to meet these standards is worthless—particularly not if it is a flower you like. It just means the flower does not meet show standards.

There are some flowers that perform well as show flowers but might not be in demand at a flower shop (some top award winners are quite traditional). There are also cult favorite dahlias that command high prices and are hard for florists and growers to keep in stock, but would not make the grade at a flower show. In some ways there are two dahlia worlds—one of show competition and another of flower lovers and floral designers who appreciate unruly blooms like 'Café au Lait'. What is popular in one world might not be in the other, though of course there is overlap. In the end, the most important thing is what *you* like and want to plant in your garden.

My heart is a garden tired
   with autumn,
Heaped with bending asters and
   dahlias heavy and dark

—SARA TEASDALE

In addition to the flower shows, ADS sponsors a series of dahlia test gardens across North America, where breeders can submit new flowers to be evaluated. The new hybrid needs to have been grown for at least three seasons, to make sure the genetics of the cross is stable and will not revert back to one of the parent flowers. You have to reserve a spot in the test gardens, as space is limited, but for a nominal fee they will grow out your dahlia to test its viability. Toward the end of the season, all test garden dahlias are evaluated by ADS judges on a point scale from 1 to 100. Dahlias that score 85 points or above are included in the CHD the following year and introduced as an officially named cultivar.

There is great excitement each spring to see the new dahlia releases for the year. Some breeders sell their introductions direct to customers, others may enter into an agreement with a commercial grower to sell the flower on their behalf. New releases tend to be expensive the first few years, as supply is limited and generally unable to meet demand. As more stock becomes available through tuber division, however, the prices come down.

COMPETITION ARRANGEMENT

FLORIST ARRANGEMENT

Making the Most of Dahlias

September is dressing herself
in show of dahlias and splendid
marigolds and starry zinnias.

—OLIVER WENDELL HOLMES

Harvesting Dahlias

Dahlias are a decorative delight, effortlessly attracting attention and lending their charms to bouquets and flower arrangements. They look equally at home bunched in a Mason jar or tin can as they do in crystal or Chinese porcelain.

Like most flowers, dahlias should be cut first thing in the morning, before the day has warmed, or in the evening once things have cooled. Because dahlias do not open much after they are picked, select blooms that are almost fully open but with no dry or withered petals (check the back to see the first layer of petals radiating out from the stem). As always, use sharp snips or scissors and clean them between plants, so as not to spread any disease that might be present.

Cut the stems just above a set of double leaves or bud (at least 12 inches down the stem). Remove all leaves along the stem and submerge in a bucket of water immediately. Dahlias do not have the longest vase life—3 to 5 days is average for purchased blooms—and proper and prompt hydration will help extend it as long as possible.

Before arranging your flowers, hold the bottom of the stems under water—in a bucket or the sink—and trim off about ½ inch, cutting on a 45-degree angle (the angle allows for maximum water absorption). Cutting under water helps to "seal" the cut and make sure it's not exposed to air as you transfer them to your vase or other receptacle. Changing the water daily, or at least every few days, will prolong their vase life, as will keeping them out of direct sunlight or unnecessary heat.

To avoid any bacterial contamination, vases used for flower arranging should be washed with detergent and a weak bleach solution. Fill vases with room-temperature water. You can add commercial flower food, or a pinch of sugar, if you choose. Any florist frogs or other wire arrangement aids that will be underwater should also be cleaned. Make sure to remove any leaves that would sit below the waterline in the vase, as they will begin to rot and shorten the life of your flowers.

Displaying Dahlias

Whether it is a simple bunch of matching blooms, a single flower in a small bud vase, or an elaborate decorative arrangement, dahlias always dazzle. Their appearance makes up for their limited vase life.

What makes the flowers so stunning is also sometimes their weakness: heavy dahlia blooms can cause stems to bend and break. For this reason, consider how you want to support the flowers. Either use a vase with a narrow neck that will allow for stems to lean and be supported or enlist some florist tricks to help along the way.

For larger arrangements using a low bowl or other receptacle, flower grids are essential. These are usually made of wire and fit into the neck or opening of a vase or other arranging vessel. They can be purchased from floral supply shops or online sellers—or you can make your own with a small bit of chicken wire, bent to fill the space (use wire cutters to cut to size). It's also possible to make lovely,

FLOWER GRID

CHICKEN WIRE

FLORAL FROG

organic-looking grids from lengths of wood or bamboo fastened in a cross pattern (use twine or flexible ties to secure the joints). If you are working with heavy stems, you may want to use a grid as well as a floral frog—a small metal disk covered in spikes that rests at the bottom of a vase or bowl and helps secure stems for greater stability. Whatever you use, make sure to affix it to the vase or vessel with florist tape or sticky clay.

Alternately, you can make a single-use grid by using tape—florist tape is ideal, but painter's tape or even clear tape should work in a pinch. Form a crisscross pattern across the neck of the receptacle that you will be using—just make sure to fill with water beforehand and dry the rim completely prior to applying tape or it will not stick properly. Once the grid is finished, insert the stems of your flowers and let the crisscross pattern help to hold them upright.

When designing a larger floral arrangement—to display on a mantlepiece or side table, for example—it's important to consider that larger dahlias will be weighty and need to be placed lower in the arrangement. Use lighter branches or decorative grasses to create size and volume in the back (ninebark, smoke bush, orache, eucalyptus, Mexican feather grass, or crab apple branches are all good contenders). Smaller, compatible flowers and leaves can fill out the middle. Dahlias mix well with other late summer blooms such as Japanese anemone, cosmos, zinnia, and bells of Ireland. Also, do not rule out mixing dahlias of different sizes, colors, and forms—simple, single-form flowers can play off larger, more elaborate blossoms with beautiful results.

In many cases dahlia arrangements are little more than a jumble of colours and shapes reminiscent of a carnival float, but they almost always just work. Dahlias . . . are so alluring in themselves, it's actually very difficult to go wrong when it comes to arranging them.

—KATHARINE WOODS

In mixed arrangements, start with the larger foliage and end by placing the dahlias. If you have a garden and want to extend the life of your arrangement, place the dahlias where they can easily be removed and replaced, and swap them out every few days for fresher blooms from the garden.

There is such variety within the dahlia genus: colors range from brilliant to blush; a geometry of shapes from round to spiky or lush with petals; the variation of size alone presents near endless options. While the flowers are easy to add to mixed arrangements, they also make stunning displays in all-dahlia bouquets (a single variety or a mix of cultivars).

Dahlias are so striking it's possible to stop the show with a single bloom in a tall, slender bottle (because the flowers can be so top-heavy, narrow-necked vessels are often needed). Imagine a long table or windowsill with a row of small glass jars or bud vases, each with a single bloom. Wide champagne coupe glasses can be used in a similar manner for an unexpected but elegant installation, and an inventive and quirky way to display ball dahlias is to hang them in the bubble-like glass spheres often used for air plants. You'll need to prop up the bloom with a bit of moss or stones to get the right angle, and add water daily, but the results can be playful and unexpected. A low bowl of waterlily dahlias floating in water is another stunning, more formal, option. Because dahlia season is so long, and the plants themselves so full of blooms, there is ample time to experiment and enjoy these generous flowers.

BALL DAHLIA IN GLASS SPHERE

SINGLE STEM IN BUD VASE

BOWL ARRANGEMENT

Edible Petals

Dahlias are edible—indeed, the tubers were used as a food crop in their native Mexico and Central America, much like a potato or Jerusalem artichoke (like Jerusalem artichokes they are high in inulin, which can be difficult to digest). While they are still sometimes used in the cuisine of Oaxaca, in southern Mexico, dahlia tubers can be stringy and sometimes even bitter. Some cultivars are thought to taste better than others, and breeders are currently working to develop more palatable hybrids, which may become commercially available in coming years. For now, however, the most fun to be had with edible dahlias comes from the petals.

The wide variety of colors in the dahlia petals lend themselves to a great many decorative uses. Make sure to use only garden grown flowers—or from a trusted source that grows organically—as commercial plants may have been treated with sprays or chemicals you would not want to consume. Petals will last 1 or 2 days after being removed from the flower heads, but it's best to store them in the refrigerator until you are ready to use them.

Here are some favorite ways to incorporate edible petals into your meals and parties:

· Top salads with dahlia petals for a bit of whimsy and color. For best effect, make sure to sprinkle on the salad *after* it has been dressed, as salad dressing will weigh down the petals and make them stick to the bowl.

- Dahlias can make a beautiful decoration for frosted cakes or cupcakes—either loose petals scattered at random or used as whole flowers for a more elaborate and artistic display (make sure to remove any full flowers before serving, as only the petals are edible). Apply petals and flowers no more than a few hours before serving.

- Freeze petals into ice cubes to be used for party drinks—either for the drinks themselves, or to fancy up a bucket for wine or champagne (just be prepared to refresh with new ice to keep it looking festive as the event goes on).

Dahlia Petal Body Scrub

Makes 2½ cups

Another way to extend the life of your flowers is to transform them into a sugar-based body scrub. One of the traditional uses of dahlia petals, going back to their earliest history, was to soothe rashes and to treat dry skin. While dahlias have no scent, you can add your own—either through using a fragrant base oil like almond or coconut, or by adding a few drops of essential oil with a scent you like. This easy scrub makes an excellent gift for friends and family.

½ cup tightly packed dahlia petals, removed from their flower heads

2 cups granulated sugar

⅔ cup base oil (either sweet almond oil, coconut oil, or a neutral oil such as grapeseed or sunflower)

5 tablespoons liquid glycerin

6 to 8 drops of essential oil (optional)

Place the fresh petals in the bowl of a food processor and add the sugar. Pulse the sugar and petal mixture in short bursts until the petals have broken down (do not let the processor run continuously). The petals should be in tiny pieces and well dispersed throughout the mixture.

Spread the sugar mixture evenly on a large baking sheet or other platter to dry (you may want to line it with a sheet of parchment paper for easier cleanup). Remove any large pieces of petal that might remain. Allow the mixture to air dry for 1 or 2 days.

Pour the sugar mixture into a large, dry bowl and mix in the oil, glycerin, and essential oil (if using). Pack into clean glass jars and keep in a cool, dry place. To use, spread on damp skin in the bath or shower and rub to exfoliate and smooth before rinsing clean (you may want to use a mesh drain insert in your bath or shower if you are concerned about bits of petal going down the drain). The scrub will last for up to 4 months.

Flower Viewing

The dahlia you brought to our isle
Your praises for ever shall speak;
Mid gardens as sweet as your smile,
And in colour as bright as your cheek.

—HENRY VASSALL FOX, THIRD BARON HOLLAND

Frances Palmer Pottery

WESTON, CONNECTICUT

What happens when an artist falls for dahlias? The result is Frances Palmer's exuberant garden and blooming career as a ceramicist. Frances was first struck by dahlias while visiting the dahlia garden in San Francisco's Golden Gate Park. The shape, color, and variety of the flowers delighted her, and she decided to add them to the garden she was designing at her new home in Connecticut. Far from city art museums, where Frances had imagined she would build her career, she began to study pottery. Over the years, both career and dahlia collection have grown. Her ceramics line focuses on vases and other flower-arranging receptacles, the shapes inspired by her flowers. In the garden, having run out of space, Frances took over a tennis court, adding raised beds. At the height of summer it is a joyous tapestry of colors and shapes, dahlias mixing with blooming amaranth and other flowers. Occasional open garden days allow for visitors, while her website and Instagram account share the beauty of a floral-inspired art journey.

FrancesPalmerPottery.com

Fiveforks Farms

UPTON, MASSACHUSETTS

When Grace Lam left a finance career in 2012, it's unlikely her family imagined they might all end up growing flowers on a 38–acre heritage farm in the rolling hills of Upton, Massachusetts, but that indeed is the story of Fivefork Farms. When Grace took the plunge into farming, her family followed. Brother Lyh-Hsin, who had been working for Habitat for Humanity, took responsibility for farm infrastructure; another brother, Lyh-Rhen, with a background in creative design, created marketing materials and took on floral design. Sisters Joyce and Lyh-Ping work off-farm, but help with financial planning, marketing, and other tasks. Parents Helen and Daniel run the greenhouse and help deliver orders for the farm's weekly flower CSA subscriptions, which routinely sell out. While the Lams grow a mixed flower farm, their dahlia program includes 30,000 plants representing more than 100 cultivars, with tuber sales as well. Not only are they growing flowers—organically, with an eye toward sustainability—they're growing a new chapter for their family as well.

FiveforkFarms.com

Summer Dreams Farm

OXFORD, MICHIGAN

Michael Genovese's agricultural roots run deep—both his grandfathers were Italian immigrants, subsistence farmers who fed their families out of backyard gardens, and he grew up watching his parents establish their own Christmas tree farm. When Michael was gifted with a few dahlia tubers by a local grower, he fell in love with flowers. The bouquets he cut elicited excitement and happiness when he gave them to friends and family. Though Michael had earned a business degree and started an office career, growing flowers soon became his calling. These days Michael's Summer Dreams Farm grows ninety different cultivars on 3½ acres in Oxford, Michigan. He's also a fierce advocate for American-grown flowers, traveling to Washington, DC, to urge lawmakers to support flower farmers (75 percent of the flowers sold in the United States are foreign-grown). Michael has a quote from his late father, Frank Genovese, printed on the back of his farm's T-shirts: "Food feeds the body, flowers feed the soul."

SummerDreamsFarm.com

Dahlia Hill

MIDLAND, MICHIGAN

The story of Dahlia Hill began in 1966, with a Mother's Day gift of dahlia tubers to Ester Breed. Her husband, Charles, planted them, not knowing that doing so would begin a fascination with the flowers that would encompass the rest of his life. Charles, a sculptor, had an art studio next to a vacant lot that sloped down to a busy intersection in Midland, Michigan. As his collection grew, Charles asked for permission to plant dahlias on the empty lot. Thus began Dahlia Hill—with 200 yards of topsoil and 1,700 tubers. It's now a volunteer-powered dahlia park that features three thousand plants of three hundred different cultivars, with the goal of presenting show-quality dahlias in a garden setting. Every summer, the hill is festooned with brightly colored flowers bursting forth from eight stone terraces. The hill also includes a memorial flower bed, where ashes can be spread. In 2018, the ashes of Ester and Charles Breed were added, after 52 years of devotion to the dahlia.

DahliaHill.org

Floret Flower Farm

SKAGIT VALLEY, WASHINGTON

It was a bouquet of sweet peas that hooked Erin Benzakein on flower farming—when she realized how flowers could bring back memories of childhood summers in a grandmother's garden. It inspired her to begin a career of making lives more beautiful through flowers. She started with 2 acres behind her Skagit Valley home north of Seattle in Washington State. Along with her flowers, Erin has now grown a company, Floret, that bridges the space between commercial growers and floral designers. She's expanded into education as well—developing tools to empower others who want to become "farmer-florists"—and is now focused on developing seeds and new dahlia cultivars. Though Floret grows a wide variety of flowers and foliage, dahlias have a special place. Through her most recent book, *Discovering Dahlias*, which celebrates the flower and the great potential in breeding new dahlias, Erin is still seeking to make life more beautiful.

FloretFlowers.com

Growing Kindness Project

CONWAY, WASHINGTON

It was a calculation error that led to the Growing Kindness Project. When aspiring flower farmer Deanna Kitchen planted more dahlias on her Twig and Vine Farm than she could reasonably sell, rather than dump the extra blooms on a compost pile, she began to pass them out—leaving bouquets at bus stops, doctor offices, and loading up a red wagon each week with her young sons and delivering buckets of blooms to a nearby retirement home. The delight of each recipient convinced Deanna of the ability of flowers to foster kindness and connection. The next year, Deanna offered tubers to anyone who wanted to grow blooms to share and the Growing Kindness Project was officially born. Starting in 2017, program members receive training in dahlia care and tubers to share in their communities. It's the generous nature of dahlias that allows for the success of the program—each plant produces dozens of blooms, and every year grows more tubers to be divided and shared.

GrowingKindnessProject.org

Swan Island Dahlias

CANBY, OREGON

If there is one place for a dahlia-lover to be on a weekend in late August or early September, it would be the rich agricultural region of the Willamette Valley in Oregon where the Gitts family tends the largest commercial dahlia farm in the United States. Named for its original location, on Portland's Swan Island, the farm has now grown to 40 acres. Each year at the end of the summer they open their flower fields for a two-weekend festival, where visitors can see 370 different cultivars in full bloom. Swan Island is now run by the second and third generations of the Gitts family, who have also spent years hybridizing dahlias, some of which carry their name—'Gitts Attention', 'Gitts Crazy', and 'Gitts Respect', among many others. If planning a visit, check the Swan Island website for operating hours. To be surrounded by so much color and beauty is a rare treat indeed.

Dahlias.com

Santa Cruz Dahlias

SANTA CRUZ, CALIFORNIA

On a quarter-acre lot on the coast of Northern California, award-winning hybridizer Kristine Albrecht is raising some of the most popular new dahlia varieties. Starting in 2006, Kristine went all in—clearing a weedy patch of land and planting five hundred tubers her first year. In addition to selling blooms to local florists, Kristine soon started hybridizing dahlias. In 2015, her first introduction—'KA's Cloud', blush-tipped white petals with hints of yellow—won both the Derrill W. Hart medal and the Lynn P. Dudley award. Subsequent introductions—'KA's Champagne', 'KA's Jubilee', and 'KA's Rosie Jo'—explore the blush and pale-pink palette so popular with florists, brides, and wedding designers, while 'KA's Kahleesi' is a massive white bloom, nearly 1 foot across, with petals that look almost like feathers. Kristine recently compiled her hybridizing knowledge into a book, *Dahlia Breeding for the Farmer-Florist and the Home Gardener*, to encourage and educate a new generation of aspiring dahlia breeders.

SantaCruzDahlias.com

KA's Champagne

Dahlia Dell

GOLDEN GATE PARK, SAN FRANCISCO

On the eastern side of Golden Gate Park's soaring white Conservatory of Flowers lies Dahlia Dell, San Francisco's public dahlia garden. In the midst of late summer, it becomes a stunning tapestry made up of all colors and forms of the flower. The garden, which is tended by volunteers from the San Francisco Dahlia Society, began in the 1980s. Tucked off the park's main drive, it is often overlooked by tourists and visitors, though the dahlia is the city flower of San Francisco. According to the official declaration, "The Dahlia partakes essentially of the character of our beloved city . . . originally Mexican, carried thence to Spain, to France and England in turn, being changed in the process from a simple daisy-like wild flower to a cosmopolitan beauty. It has come back to San Francisco, like the sophisticated world traveler it is, to find its favorite home here, where it thrives in the cool summers and the moist air of our fog-swept, sandy gardens by the sea."

GoldenGatePark.com/dahlia-dell-garden-in-golden-gate-park.html

The Happy Dahlia Farm

PETALUMA, CALIFORNIA

Meagan Major says intuition brought her to the 3-acre property on the outskirts of Petaluma, an hour north of San Francisco. When a friend fell in love with a woman who was looking to sell her dahlia farm, Meagan knew it was meant for her (she had secretly looked up flower farming jobs a few months prior but had grown discouraged when people laughed and said she was crazy for considering it). She and her husband, Tony, had been dreaming of a place where they could hold events and which would serve as a healing force in the community—she just didn't know it would be a flower farm. But when she stood among sixty thousand dahlia tubers, Meagan said yes. That was the beginning of the Happy Dahlia Farm, which sells cut flowers, tubers, and plants—and includes a space for workshops, classes, and special events held among the thousands of dahlia plants all growing in rainbow order. Clearly it was meant to be.

TheHappyDahliafarm.com

Charlie McCormick

DORSET, ENGLAND

The most photogenic dahlia border of all time—at least the most photogenic border on the internet—belongs to Charlie McCormick. The New Zealand–born florist and gardener has transformed the garden of an 1820s parsonage in Dorset in southern England—where he lives with his husband, interior designer Ben Pentreath—into a tapestry of color and shape. The dahlia border shines in lavender, dark red, coral, and peach, and has made fast fans of Charlie's large Instagram following. The border, made up of about 150 tubers, is unstudied elegance. While many dahlia gardens can overwhelm with clashing tones, this one is a seemingly effortless mix of shapes and colors. In the often-foggy mornings of an English early autumn, the colors glow with a certain luminosity. Other flower beds, in the nearby vegetable garden, provide the blooms Charlie likes to enter in local agricultural fairs—a practice that dates back to his childhood in New Zealand and which regularly earns him ribbons and certificates.

Instagram.com/mccormickcharlie

Ferncliff Gardens

MISSION, BRITISH COLUMBIA, CANADA

Any avid dahlia grower in North America likely knows
the Ferncliff name—either through the nursery, Ferncliff
Gardens, which has been providing high-quality dahlia
tubers for the last hundred years, or via the dozens of dahlia
hybrids they've introduced—such as 'Ferncliff Copper',
'Ferncliff Bliss', 'Ferncliff Illusion', and so many more. All this
is the work of David and Shelia Jack, who are continuing a
family legacy. David's grandfather Milton started the nursery
as a gladioli farm in the 1920s. After earning a horticulture
degree in Ontario, David returned to the family farm, located
east of Vancouver in British Columbia, and has been breeding dahlias ever since. A visit in late summer promises a
chance to see the display garden planted with row upon row
of colors and shapes (more than 150 different cultivars), and
to order Ferncliff tubers for the following spring. And if you
see any young girls running through the gardens, it's likely
David and Shelia's granddaughters, the fifth generation of
this flower farming family.

FerncliffGardens.com

Gerrie Hoek

Glossary

ANEMONE: dahlia form that features a ring of flat petals around a center of elongated florets.

ANTHER: the end portion of a flower stamen that produces pollen.

BALL: perfectly round dahlia flower form featuring evenly spaced petals, also available in miniature ball (2–3½ inches) and pompon (under 2 inches) size.

CACTUS: dahlia form featuring rolled spiky petals (see also *semi-cactus*, *incurved cactus*, and *laciniated*).

COLLARETTE: dahlia form featuring an outer ring of peals and an inner "collar" of shorter petals around an open center.

CROSS: the process of hybridizing plants by cross-pollinating and growing out the seed that is produced.

CULTIVAR: a plant intentionally created through breeding, not found in the wild.

DEADHEADING: removing withered flowers from a plant after it has bloomed.

EYES: plant buds located on a root or tuber.

FORMAL DECORATIVE: dahlia form featuring double blooms with broad, blunt-tipped petals that curve back toward the stem. Formal decorative have evenly placed petals (see also *informal decorative*).

HYBRID: a plant cultivar created by crossing two parent plants to pass on specific desirable traits.

INCURVED: dahlia petals whose tips curve slightly back toward the center of the bloom.

INCURVED CACTUS: dahlia form similar to cactus, with rolled petals that are spiky but curve back toward the center of the bloom.

INFORMAL DECORATIVE: dahlia form featuring double blooms with flat petals that roll at the tips (see also *formal decorative*).

LACINIATED: dahlia form similar to cactus with the same spiky, rolled petals, but each petal forks in two at the tip.

MIGNON (OR MIGNON SINGLES): similar to single dahlias, mignon singles feature a single row of petals around an open center. Mignon singles measure less than 2 inches across and have rounded tips.

NOVELTY DOUBLE: catch-all category for dahlias that do not fit other forms; novelty double have closed centers (see also *novelty open*).

NOVELTY OPEN: catch-all category for dahlias that do not fit other forms; novelty open have open centers (see also *novelty double*).

ORCHID: dahlia form that features eight rolled petals around an open center and resembles a star.

ORCHETTE: dahlia form similar to orchid with eight rolled petals and the addition of a petaloid collar around the open center.

PEONY: dahlia form that features an open center and several rows of slightly cupped petals.

POMPON: round dahlia of the ball form but less than 2 inches in diameter.

SEMI-CACTUS: dahlia form similar to cactus, with petals that are slightly broader at the base.

SINGLES (OR SINGLE DAHLIAS): dahlia form that features a single row of petals around an open center.

SPECIES: original form of dahlia, featuring a single row of petals and an open center.

STAMEN: male reproductive portion of a plant, located in the center of the flower; made up of the anther (upper, pollen-bearing portion) and the filament (stem on which the anther rests).

STELLAR: double dahlia form that features slightly creased petals that curve backward and away from the center.

STIGMA: portion of the reproductive system of a flower; where the pollen is collected and germinates.

STYLE: portion of the reproductive system of a flower, the style connects the ovary and the stigma, where the pollen is collected.

VARIETY: naturally occurring plant or flower that grows true to form; not an intentionally cultivated or hybridized version.

WATERLILY: dahlia form that features broad, shallow petals that curve inward at the tips.

Snowflake

UMBELLIFER FLOWERS & DAHLIAS

Pests & Diseases

APHIDS: Tiny insects—less than ¼ inch—that suck the nutrients out of plants. Aphids multiply quickly, looking like a gray-green crust. Sometimes they appear white, black, brown, green, yellow, or gray. Aphids like the juicy new plant growth and will generally hide on the underside of leaves. Small aphid infestations may be remedied with a blast of water from a hose several times a week, or by hand picking (make sure to destroy removed leaves, which harbor aphid eggs). Or try spraying plants with a solution of water and a few drops of dish soap. For more persistent infections, applications of neem oil, insecticidal soap, and horticultural oils have all proved successful.

Be proactive about warding off aphids by cultivating plants from the Umbelliferae family—parsley, carrots, fennel, sweet cicely, white lace flower, and more. Umbellifers attract hoverflies and lacewings, which feed on aphids. Carrots, in particular, when left unharvested, have lacy white flowers that float on long, tall stems and look lovely between the dahlia blooms.

BOTRYTIS BLIGHT: Browned or blackened areas on your dahlia plant (stem, leaf, or bud) is likely the work of *Botrytis paeoniae,* which overwinters in plants from the previous summer. The blight releases spores in the spring rains to infect the new growth from that year. Young shoots may rot off entirely. Older infections may develop a gray fuzz on top of the infected areas. If an infection is found, remove promptly and burn or dispose of in the garbage (not a home composting system).

CUCUMBER BEETLES: Measuring only ¼ inch and yellow-green with a black head and eleven black spots on its curved back, cucumber beetles are reminiscent of ladybugs. Though tiny, they can have a destructive impact on dahlias and other plants, as they eat small holes in the leaves, stems, and roots. A dahlia with a cucumber beetle infestation can seem to whither and get raggedy before your eyes. It's hard to handpick these tiny beetles, because they quickly fly away or drop to the ground and hide. Chemical controls are not recommended for cucumber beetles—any pesticides will also harm the local bee population—but they can be captured in a homemade trap made by spreading a yellow plastic cup with insect glue. Mount the cups to a garden stake. Traps can be baited with a cotton ball scented with clove oil, which attract the beetles. Alternately, spread a light-colored sheet around the infected plants and shake, collecting and destroying any dislodged beetles.

CUCUMBER BEETLE

CUTWORM: What a heartbreak it can be to check your dahlias in the morning and find the tender emerging shoots cut off at the stem. If this happens, it may be the work of cutworms, which grow to 1.75 inches long and are grayish-black or brown. If you find your new dahlia shoots cut down at the base, dig around in the soil with your finger to see if you can find the culprit and dispose of it. This will be most successful first thing in the morning. Another option is to treat with a slug bait (look for a brand that is safe for children and pets), which includes iron phosphate and spinosad, and can be used to protect against earwigs as well.

DEER: Do deer eat dahlias? They can and they may. Whether or not they eat your dahlias depends on the type of deer, the deer population, and what other food sources are available. If you have deer issues, it's best to take precautions. This can run from fencing your dahlia patch to planting other plants that deer like better in the hope that they fill up on those. The good news is that dahlias are not a favorite of deer, but there is always the danger they might look good to a particular deer on a particular day.

EARWIGS: Glossy, flat insects of reddish brown that can grow up to 1 inch long, earwigs are easy to recognize due to the curved pinchers attached to the rear of their abdomens. While earwigs do beneficial things in the garden—eat mites, aphids, and undesirable nematodes, and are helpful in compost piles—they may also eat your dahlias. Earwig protection includes spreading diatomaceous earth around the base of dahlias, putting out damp crumpled newspaper or cardboard for them to shelter in as a trap (dispose of any earwigs caught in soapy water), or spreading a sheet or tarp around the base of the plants and gently shaking the stalks to dislodge any earwigs.

LEAFHOPPERS: Known for their acrobatics, leafhoppers are tiny, wedge-shaped insects, able to pierce dahlias and suck out the content of surface plant cells. This results in stippling on the leaves, yellowing, or curling. If you rustle a dahlia plant and tiny insects jump or fly off, it's likely you have a leafhopper infestation. Ladybugs and lacewings are natural predators for leafhoppers, so providing habitat to encourage their numbers (see entry for *aphids*) can be helpful. In case of infestation, make a trap out of a yellow plastic cup (see entry for cucumber beetles). Alternately, treat with diatomaceous earth or spray with insecticidal soap, making sure to spray the underside of leaves.

MITES: Tiny arachnids about the size of a grain of sand, spider mites leave thin strands of silk webbing behind and damage dahlia leaves by piercing and sucking their cell contents. This first appears as a light stippling on the leaves, which then turn yellow or reddish and drop off. Dusty and dry conditions may cause outbreaks of spider mites, so irrigate appropriately. Finally, a water spray may be helpful in dislodging spider mites; make sure to get the underside of leaves. If more help is needed, add an insecticidal soap or neem oil to the spray.

MOSAIC VIRUS (OR TOBACCO MOSAIC VIRUS): Dahlia leaves with pale-green or yellow streaks along the veins, or stunted, rolled, or twisted leaves may be suffering from this virus. It resembles mite damage, but it will affect the entire plant. Mosaic virus is spread by aphids when they pierce the stem or leaves to feed on the sap. While the virus cannot be spread to surrounding dahlias if there are no aphids to transport it, there is also no cure; the plant must be removed and destroyed. Prevent this virus by being vigilant against aphid infestation (see entry for *aphids*).

POWDERY MILDEW: A white or grayish bloom on leaves and stem, powdery mildew is a common fungal infection, especially late in the summer. It is unsightly but will not generally harm the plant. If the leaves seem otherwise healthy under the whitish bloom, it's fine to leave them until regular end of summer removal. If the leaves are withering, cut back to the base and dispose of them (not in a home composting system). Prevent powdery mildew through standard good practices: plant dahlias with adequate spacing for airflow, remove weeds, avoid overhead watering systems, and water early in the day.

ROOT GALL (ALSO CALLED ROOT KNOT): Caused by an infection of root knot nematodes. This is usually discovered when a dahlia grower digs up their tubers at the end of the season. If you find feeder roots that show galls—lumps that range in size—it is likely you have an infection. The lumps contain female nematodes and the entire plant should be removed and destroyed (do not compost it). Because root gall nematodes also infest the surrounding soil, and can easily infect most vegetable and ornamental plants, the best thing is to not grow dahlias in that spot again. Plant grass, which is not susceptible to nematodes, for 3 to 4 years to break the cycle (it's fine to plant dahlias in other parts of your garden, just keep them as far as you can from the infected site).

SLUGS, SNAILS: If you are growing dahlias, you will encounter slug or snails—usually when the shoots first emerge. Because damage from slugs and snails can significantly delay dahlia growth, an application of slug bait is recommended as soon as shoots emerge early in the season (look for a brand that is safe for pets and children). Check the bait every few days for the first 3 to 4 weeks and reapply as needed. It is possible to see leaf damage later in the season. If that is the case, look on the underside of leaves in the evening when it is easiest to catch slugs and snails. They are a nuisance, but a minor one.

THRIPS: These tiny insects of the order Thysanoptera suck the liquid out of plant tissue, resulting in scarring, discoloration, and dead areas. Thrips tend to attack drought-stressed or otherwise weakened plants. Any infected branches or buds should be removed immediately and disposed of in the garbage (not compost). There are no preventative measures, apart from good plant health and hygiene, but residential growers report success with insecticidal soap or neem oil. Chemical controls are not recommended for the backyard grower.

VERTICILLIUM WILT: A soil-based fungal disease that thrives in the damp and cool, verticillium wilt infects through the roots and clogs the tissues (xylem) that the plant relies on to transport water. This causes wilting and yellowing that can turn brown as the plant dies. If these leaves drop to the ground they can spread the fungus. If infection occurs, plants should be removed as soon as possible and disposed of (not composted). That area should not be replanted with dahlias; choose a different crop that is not prone to verticillium wilt infections.

Jowey Nicky

Resources

Dahlia growing can easily become a passion—a few years in and you may be ripping up your lawn and trying to track down hard-to-find tubers to complete your collection. Avid growers refer to it as an obsession, but certainly it's a positive one: encouraging physical activity, time outdoors, and the benefit of gorgeous flowers to share. Obsessed or not, here are some resources to help you along the way.

Societies and General Resources

AMERICAN DAHLIA SOCIETY (ADS)

The US-based dahlia society for North America, ADS sponsors the test garden network, publishes the annual Classification and Handbook of Dahlias (CHD), and serves as the parent organization for seventy or so local dahlia chapters across the continent.

Dahlia.org

BRITISH NATIONAL DAHLIA SOCIETY (NDS)

Founded in 1881, the NDS is one of the world's largest all-dahlia societies. A sponsor for several annual flower shows and conferences, NDS publishes yearly bulletins, classification guides, and more.

Dahlia-NDS.co.uk

DAHLIA ADDICT

One of the best tools for the dahlia grower, this site serves as a database of dahlia suppliers. Here you can search by cultivar name, and each entry will list the suppliers known to carry that tuber (along with price). If you are trying to find the name of a mystery flower you have seen in another garden, you can search by size and color. Dahlia Addict also has one of the most comprehensive lists of dahlia growers and resellers in North America. If you are looking to build up your stock of tubers, or trying to locate or identify a rare flower, this is the place to seek it out.

DahliaAddict.com

Dahlia Suppliers

Arrowhead Dahlias
PO Box 814
Platteville, CO 80651
970-396-5046
ArrowheadDahlias.com

Creekside Growers
692 Windham Rd. 11 RR2
Delhi, Ontario ON N4B 2W5
Canada
905-746-9253
CreeksideGrowers.ca

Dahlia Shed
644 E. Main Rd.
Middletown, RI 02842
dahliashed@gmail.com
DahliaShed.com

Ferncliff Gardens
35344 McEwen Ave.
Mission, BC V2V 6R4
Canada
604-826-2447
FerncliffGardens.com

Happy Dahlia Farm
2478 E Washington St.
Petaluma, CA 94954
707-338-9478
TheHappyDahliaFarm.com

Old House Dahlias
11600 S. US 101
Tillamook, OR 97141
503-771-1199
OldHouseDahlias.com

Stone Meadow Gardens
2273 Hwy. 3A
Castlegar, BC V1N 4P1
Canada
250-304-8084
StoneMeadowGardens.ca

Summer Dreams Farm
4780 Seymour Lake Rd.
Oxford, MI 48371
248-802-8979
SummerDreamsFarm.com

**Sunny Meadows
Flower Farm**
3555 Watkins Rd.
Columbus, OH 43232
614-570-6719
SunnyMeadowsFlower
Farm.com

Swan Island
PO Box 700
Canby, OR 97013
800-410-6540
Dahlias.com

Further Reading

Dahlia Breeding for the Farmer-Florist and the Home Gardener, by Kristine Albrecht (Independently published, 2020).

Dahlias: Beautiful Varieties for Home and Garden, by Naomi Slade, photographer Georgianna Lane (Gibbs Smith, 2018).

Discovering Dahlias, by Erin Benzakein (Chronicle Books, 2021).

Encyclopedia of Dahlias, by Bill McClaren (Timber Press, 2009).

Nijinsky

Fairway Spur

TARA AUSTEN WEAVER is an award-winning writer, editor, and avid gardener. She is author of several books, including *Orchard House* (finalist for the 2016 Washington State Book Awards), *Growing Berries and Fruit Trees in the Pacific Northwest*, and the Little Book of Flowers series. She is trained as a Permaculture Designer, Master Gardener, and Master Composter/Soil Builder. Tara writes frequently about gardening, agriculture, food, art, travel, and social justice. More information can be found on TaraWeaver.com.

EMILY POOLE was born and raised in the mountain town of Jackson Hole, Wyoming. After receiving her BFA in illustration from the Rhode Island School of Design, she returned west to put down roots in the mossy hills of Oregon. She can be found exploring tidepools and cliffsides, gathering inspiration, and making artwork about our fellow species and how to be better neighbors with them.

Printed in China

SASQUATCH BOOKS with colophon is a registered trademark of Penguin Random House LLC

26 25 24 23 22   9 8 7 6 5 4 3 2 1

Illustrations: Emily Poole | Editor: Hannah Elnan
Production editor: Jill Saginario | Designer: Anna Goldstein

Library of Congress Cataloging-in-Publication Data
Names: Weaver, Tara Austen, author.
Title: Dahlias : a little book of flowers / Tara Austen Weaver.
Description: Seattle, WA : Sasquatch Books, 2022.
Identifiers: LCCN 2021002931 | ISBN 9781632173614 (hardcover)
Subjects: LCSH: Dahlias.
Classification: LCC SB413.D13 W43 2022 | DDC 635.9/33983—dc23
LC record available at https://lccn.loc.gov/2021002931K]

Grateful acknowledgment is made to the following:
Page 15: Courtesy of Bryn Gribben. "Dahlia," first published in
Passengers Journal. Reprinted by permission by the author.

ISBN: 978-1-63217-361-4

Sasquatch Books
1904 Third Avenue, Suite 710
Seattle, WA 98101

SasquatchBooks.com